Seven Steps of Faith
Traveling with God

*A Belief Guide to Faith & Transformation Learn How
to Receive the Unwavering Assurance of Faith*

Margret V. Oglesby
Traveling With William H. Anderson Jr.

Seven Steps of Faith Traveling with God
Keeping the Faith!

PROMINENT
BOOKS
EDGE

5830 E 2nd St, Ste 7000 #9983
Casper, WY 82609
USA

Have Faith

Have faith my sister life long
Not for the swift, but for the strong
It takes willpower and determination
Love, zeal for life and imagination

Don't settle for mediocrity
Claim your total victory
God's wisdom and peace is liberating
Soar with exhilaration

Be still and know that I am God!
Let go and let God be in charge
Ask God for wisdom,
understanding and power
He is my high tower

Less of me, but more of God
I'm a new person in Him from the heart
I worship and praise Him for who HE IS
According to God's will

Written by Margret V. Oglesby

"How beautiful upon the mountains are the feet of Him who brings good news, who publishes peace, who brings good news of happiness, who publishes salvation, who says to Zion, "Your God reigns" Isaiah 52:7

Dedication

*Dedicated to my daughter, Angela V. Coburn, and
four sisters: Joetta Powell, Mary Gordon,
Wilma Lambert, Bertha Stanley and to
my loving and faithful mother, Veessa Oglesby*

This book is dedicated to the women in my life who gave
much and lived the unwavering assurance of faith. They
achieved power from the inner strength given freely through
God's grace – moving forward by faith and courage. These
courageous and beautiful women have walked by faith
and not by sight in many situations known – yet adhering
to the strong belief principles of trusting God.

**This small book also reflects my personal journey traveling
with Sgt William Anderson Jr. as we traveled with God
Stepping Out on Faith – walking with a poetic heart.**
*"Keep alert, stand firm in your faith, be courageous, be strong.
Let all that you do be done in love."* – 1 Corinthians 16:13-14

~~~

Unless specified or stated differently, all scripture quotations
are taken from the Old and New Testament of God's Promises
Edition of King James Version (KJV) of the Holy Bible.
Copyright – 1998 Keepsake Promise Bible, INC

Acknowledgements

I am so thankful & grateful for all the encouragement and support received from my family and friends. I truly love and appreciate all of you so much! I thank God for surrounding me with inspiring & positive people that has given me the confidence and courage to write this book – and especially to Sgt William (Bill) Anderson Jr. who traveled with me on this journey. Bill has been my strength during some weak times in my life. *I thank God for accepting me just as I am with all my faults.* A Special Shout-Out goes also to the Anderson family!

In the book of Genesis – chapter 1:22-24, said that Enoch "Walked with God" for 365 years. I believe that it is no coincident there are 365 days in a year, and to me my two brothers (Enoch and White Oglesby) – symbolizes God's Blessings of Love, Godliness & Spirituality. Amen

Meditate on this thought that we should always "travel with God" everyday!

Table of Contents

Seven Steps of Faith

Joe and Veessa Oglesby's seven children: Bertha, Margret,
White, Wilma, Enoch, Mary and Joetta

"Now faith is the substance of things hoped for, the evidence of things not seen…. Through faith, we understand that the worlds were framed by the word of God, so that things which are seen were not made of things which do appear… But without faith it is impossible to please Him: for he that cometh to God must believe that he is, and that he is a rewarder of them that diligently seek Him." – Hebrews 11:1, 3, 6

For we walk by faith, not by sight."
2 Corinthians 5:7

Meaning of Stepping Out on Faith

Stepping out on faith means releasing ALL to God and letting Him do the rest. This is very hard to do for most people. Why is this? Because we live in a culture that puts high value on independence and *"doing your own thing."* However, when we truly let go, we give up something – our own self-control that we have often felt very proud of. Why would anyone want to step out on faith when they feel they have accomplished all things on their own? This false sense of independence means we must become **dependent on God** in order to release this false controlling power to Him.

"Let us hold on firmly to the hope we profess, because we can trust God to keep his promise." – Hebrews 10:23 (GNT)

Every **step** we take in life, God is with us. He said, *"Never will I leave you and never will I forsake you" (Hebrews 13:5).* Every journey begins by taking that first step. You can begin by walking in faith – depending on God. Early one morning while I was praying, **God identified to me these seven steps of faith.** Although walking is a natural process, it takes commitment to step with Confidence, Assurance and Trust

(called faith). If you never take that first step, you'll never experience the fullness of God. In this little book, you will experience God in a special way as you walk through the sevens step of faith. Take each step inch by inch.

Step one: <u>*accepting God*</u> – when you accept God in your life, you are beginning a partnership with Him. Often that first step is the hardest yet most rewarding since it requires you making a deep conscious and emotional change. This is when you are making a commitment to God in faith.

God is awesome! His love for you will never change. Even when you are in doubt, you can come to Him. When you make that first step in faith, you are beginning to accept God.

Step two: _forgiveness of sin_ – by asking God for forgiveness of your sins, something miraculous happens in your life. True healing begins.

Step three: _releasing to God_ – by letting Him take control of your life. Let go. God will provide you with all your needs. *"And my God will meet all your needs according to his glorious riches in Christ Jesus"* *(Philippians 4:19).* Your reward is happiness, victory, love, joy, and peace in all areas of your lives.

Step four: _trusting God_ – by faith to work out all things for your good. *"He who trusts in the Lord will prosper. He who trusts in himself is a fool" (Proverb 28:25-26).* He simply wants us to accept Him in our lives, release our needs to Him, and then trust Him to do just that.

Step five: _transformation_ – is where you begin to revolutionize and change your lifestyle. Here you make changes in the way you think, feel, and

act about all things. You begin to celebrate life. What a celebration it is!

Step six: _praising God_ – in all things. Hallelujah is the highest praise. This is real worship for He is worthy to be praised. As Byron Cage wrote: *"Praise Him in the morning, Praise Him in the noonday. Praise Him when the sun goes down!"*

The final step seven: _keeping the faith_ – when all things are released to God (every plan, every challenge, every circumstance or responsibility), you will experience exhilarating inner peace and confidence beyond measures. This means we no longer have to carry our burdens on our shoulders (weighing us down), but giving them to Him. As we step out on faith (putting our trust in Him), we believe without a doubt that God has already moved on it. It is done! God has the final word – the end.

"For by grace given me I say to every one of you; Do not think of yourself more highly than you ought, but rather think of yourself with sober judgment, in accordance with the measure of faith God has given you." Romans 12:3 KJV

"She considers a field and buys it; with the fruit of her hands, she plants a vineyard … She opens her mouth with wisdom and the teaching of kindness is on her tongue." – Proverbs 31:16, 26

"Let us hold on firmly to the hope we profess, because we can trust God to keep his promise." – Hebrews 10:23 (GNT)

"Looking unto Jesus, the author and finisher of our faith; who for the joy that was set before Him endured the cross, despising the shame, and is set down on the right hand of the throne of God." – Hebrews 12:2

"But without faith it is impossible to please Him: for he that cometh to God must believe that he is, and that he is a rewarder of them that diligently seek Him." – Hebrews 11:6

> *"This little book is about making small steps of faith moving toward a more fulfilling and happier life."*

People Global Anthem

World peace, diversity, love and harmony
Joy, praise, surrendering to God's victory One
God, one nation, one love for all!
Understanding true knowledge of God's call
One God, one nation, one love for all!

God bless us all, the world that we love, Omnipotent
gift of grace from above. Created to be free,
We begin our true journey …

We step forward in faith.
No more wars – no more hate. People meeting
horrible faith, Mothers no more weeping, Fathers
no more creeping, Babies no more tears,
These are the blesseth years.

Deeply rooted faith in God, Open your heart.
Eliminate adversity,
Heart, soul, truth and reality. With spiritual
surrendering, We claim our true inheritance.
We proclaim our faith in God's divine plan, Together we
stand to salute our global nation. Nothing is impossible, if
only we believe, Have faith the size of a mustard seed.
Stop destruction, deprivation and retaliation cease,

Forgive us as we learn to live in peace. Embracing God's divine plan,
Sheltering in His protective hand, Blessing His magnificent land.
God bring us to live in peace.

Celebrate global patriotic triumph – revolution,
Rainbow colors for strong heritage – tradition.
Declare independence from hunger and strife,

Prayerfully commemorate all human rights.

No ground one, but world one,
From trials and tribulations – you can't run!
Thy kingdom come; Thy Will be done.
On earth, as in heaven, for our global nation.
Reaching out to all people in prayer.
Take refuge for GOD IS always there!

Written in 2001 by Margret V. Oglesby

Note from the author and songwriter:
After reflecting on September 11,2001 catastrophes, God inspired and guided me to write this song "People Global Anthem" and I had it produced on CD. Music and Song performed by Minister Larry Rodgers.

This is where it all started...

Joe and Veessa Oglesby

These are two beautiful Souls that truly loved God, their family and community

The Making of a New Milestone Along the Journey

We are honoring two remarkable and pro-
found people who have had an incredible
influence in our lives. They were the epit-
ome of strength, courage and wisdom, but
mostly, love. They remain a beacon of light
to guide and comfort us whenever our path
is dark. It is in their footsteps that we so
gracefully trod; it is in their memories that
we always cherish. We are talking about
the two who started it all – our parents.

Although this year, 2024, marks our 50th
Oglesby Family reunion, it was in 1974 after the death of our father,
Joe Nathan Oglesby, that we got started. This was also the year that
we came together to celebrate our mother, Veessa Oglesby's 62nd
birthday and realized the need for our eighteen children to get to
know each other better. While they were young, we wanted them to
grow up knowing their cousins and feeling a sense of belonging to
an extended family. What better way to strengthen family ties than
a family reunion.

Over the years these reunions have become a source of great pride
and fun memories--from adventuring around the country, sampling
the best home- cooked meals, to sharing the photos and videos
of events. Now, without those memories, I wonder what our lives
would be like ---a lot would be missing. For example, there is a
chance we may not know names, people, places, where they are from,
or to whom they belong. Even worse, we may not care enough to
know. We are talking about the impact of these reunions on 2 or 3

generations! That is a long time to keep something going, but the benefits have been well worth the efforts.

I believe Mama and Daddy would feel very honored to know their seven children have each done their part to set a good example in keeping our family legacy going strong all these years. Now, as we become the elders, as we slow down with age, as we pass on the torch, we can be assured and hopeful that our children will also feel the passion to give our legacy a new breath of life--a passion to hope, a passion to dream, to believe, to achieve, and to carry the torch of enlightenment on and on for generations to come.

Written by Bertha Oglesby –
a teacher, a visionarian, a philanthropist

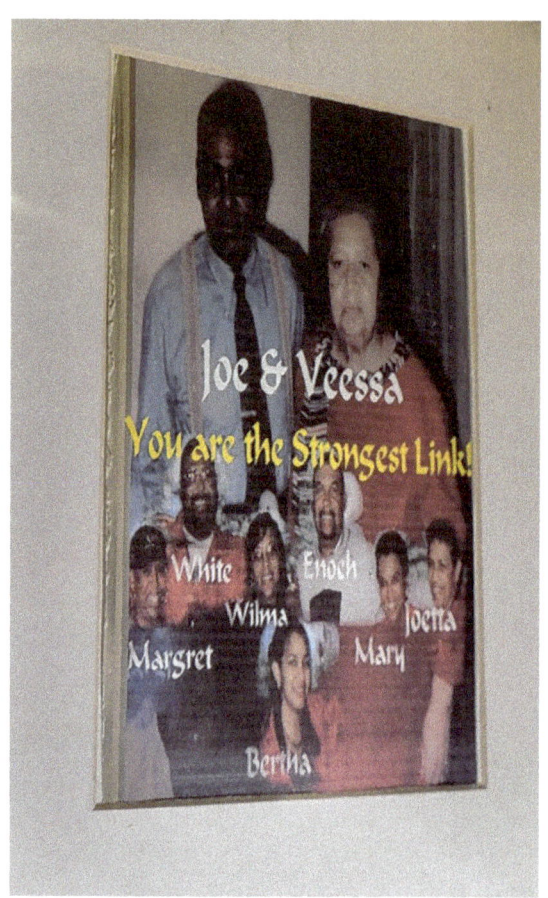

Joe and Veessa Oglesby's seven children: Bertha, Margret, White, Wilma, Enoch, Mary and Joetta

PART ONE

Seven Steps of Faith

"Now faith is the substance of things hoped for, the evidence of things not seen... Through faith we understand that the worlds were framed by the word of God, so that things which are seen were not made of things which do appear... But without faith it is impossible to please him: for he that cometh to God must believe that he is, and that he is a rewarder of them that diligently seek him." – Hebrews 11:1, 3, 6

"And Jesus answering saith unto them, Have faith in God. For verily I say unto you, that whosoever shall say unto this mountain be thou removed, and be thou cast into the sea; and shall not doubt in his heart but shall believe that those things which he saith shall come to pass; he shall have whatsoever he saith." Mark 11:22-23

What is your mountain today? As soon as you plant your mustard seed of faith in God, your mountains become His responsibility – and you can then rest in His faithfulness.

First Step of Faith: Accepting God

"I am the gate; whoever enters through me will be saved; He will come in and go out and find pasture." – John 10:9 NIV

When you accept God in your life, you are taking on a partnership with Him. You are getting into God. You learn of God through His Word (Bible). *Remember the word unto thy servant, upon which thou hast caused me to hope (Psalm 119:49 KJV)*. The Bible is your roadmap to life. It is God's words for living. It will tell you the right direction, things to avoid, and ways to improve your life. Whatever direction He leads you on this journey, God is your provider (Jehovah Jireh). He guides you through the bumps in your road, the turns in your life, and the up and downs on your path. The Bible has endured through centuries of testing. Through it all, He says stay in my Word (Bible), come to Me and I will direct your life. *"And they that know thy name will put their trust in thee; for thou, Lord, hast not forsaken them that seek thee."*
– Psalm 9:10

God has given you "free-will" to choose what path to travel. The decision or choice is always yours. You must be willing to accept God's plan and allow Him to lead you. When you accept God in your life, you are born again in Christ.

"Marvel not that I said unto thee, Ye must be born again." – John 3:7.

Being born again in Christ, you are His and not the world's. God can do anything but fail. He will perform miracles in your life. He will help you to see the truth and beauty of each day as you share His love with others. As you do this, you will notice a paradigm change in your thinking and quality of life. You will smile and not frown. You will have joy, peace and confidence in all things. *"Do not fear, for I am with you, do not be afraid, for I am your God; I will strengthen you, I will help you, I will uphold you with my victorious right hand." –* Isaiah 41:10

By accepting God in your life, you are going into a covenant with Him. *"In all thy ways acknowledge Him, and he shall direct thy paths"* *(Proverbs 3:6 KJV).* You are also accepting God's plan of good for your life. Over 2000 years ago, God gave us a very special gift when

He sent His one and only Son Jesus to the earth to walk and talk with us. Jesus adopted us as His very own. *"Thy faithfulness is unto all generations: thou hast established the earth, and it abideth." – Psalm 119:90 KJV.* He shed His blood for us (covenant) so that we could share in life and death this gift. *"God is not a man, that He should lie; neither the son of man, that he should repent: hath he said, and shalt he not do it? Or hath he spoken, and shall he not make it good?" – Numbers 23:19.*

Q & A

1. The _____ is your roadmap to life.
2. God has given you "_____" to choose what path you travel.
3. By accepting God in your life, you are going into a _____ with Him.

Footstep Prayer:
Heavenly Father, I thank You for accepting me just as I am with all my faults. Amen.

Accepting God
"My Prayer Warriors"

I believe that prayer is necessary for us to experience spiritual growth. No matter what your sins or transgressions (indulgence, resentment, manipulation, wrong-doing, offense or crime, failure, jealousy, self-ishness or just a bad attitude) or to whom you have sinned, know that through God's Grace, He has already forgiven you. Just ask in a simple prayer or meditate with the Lord's Prayer.

Spend time talking to God everyday!

The Lord's Prayer
Our Father, Who art in heaven, hallowed be Thy Name.
Thy kingdom come, thy will be done On earth as it is in heaven.
Give us this day our daily bread, And forgive us our debts,
As we forgive our debtors.
And lead us not into temptation, But deliver us from evil,
For Thine is the kingdom
And the power, and the glory, forever. Amen.

— Matthew 6:9-13

Simply tell God all about it. He knows it anyway. He encourages us to talk (pray) to Him. With Him, you can express your desires, hopes, and dreams. When you ask God for forgiveness, something miraculous happens in your life. This is when true healing begins. No matter how large or small your sins, He will forgive you. It is not based on size or degree. Yes, *ALL SIN*, even if your sins are for lying, cheating, disrespecting, or mentally hurting another human being, He will forgive you and others. Just ask! "*If you forgive anyone, I also forgive him. And what I have forgiven – if there was anything to forgive – I have forgiven in the sight of Christ for your sake." – 2 Corinthians 2:10*

He is nonjudgmental. No chastisement. He has no discipline, punishment, rebuke, scolding or reprimand. He is God and God is love. He is compassionate.

"Therefore, I say unto you, what things so ever ye desire, when ye pray, believe that ye receive them, and ye shall have them. And when ye stand praying, forgive, if ye have ought against any: that your Father also which is in heaven may forgive you your trespasses. But if ye do not forgive, neither will your Father which is in heaven forgive your trespasses." – Mark 11:24-26.

Q & A
1. How do you define prayer?
2. Are you reassured that your prayers will be answered?

Footstep Prayer:
Heavenly Father, I thank you for forgiveness of all my sins knowingly and unknowingly. Amen.

Prayer for a Friend

I asked God to bless my friend,
as I prayed for her today to guide, protect and strengthen her
as she travels along life's way...

God's love and mercy are with you
His Word is always true
And when His Arms embraces you, just
know He will see you through.

I asked God to strengthen you that you might achieve insight.
I asked God for your good health that you might enjoy life.
I asked God to give you wisdom and the happiness it will bring

I asked God to give you power that you might do great things.

So, journey the road you're traveling Be grateful and richly blessed
Remember that GOD loves you Be still and let Him do the rest.

Despite myself my spoken and unspoken
prayers are heard and answered.

Written by Margret V. Oglesby
Dedicated to Minister Ardella James

Time Out

When life challenges your patience, courage and faith
When lessons learned leave a stain of despair embraced, **time out!**

When you think that your only inspiration is to dream
When it seems that your flowers don't bloom
in season or it seems, **time out!**

When it seems hope and joy are gone Then the sun
appears to shines only in your neighbor's yard
Be on guard that God is in charge
Time out and take a God break!

When God allows you to hear the birds sing
And you feel His breeze on your face
When you hear His small voice You are in His presence so Rejoice!
Take a God break!

God will use mysterious others to brighten your day
And strangers unaware to radiate life-affirming hope and faith

When God puts people in your life to encourage your daily race
He allows you to feel His loving arms through their positive embrace

Know that God will be with you always
Giving you His Amazing Grace!

Embrace God's love!

Written by Margret V. Oglesby May 8, 2014

Second Step of Faith: Forgiveness

"For if ye forgive men their trespasses, your heavenly Father will also forgive you." –
Matthew 6:14

"The Lord has heard my supplications; The Lord accepts my prayer." – *Psalm 6:9.*

The step of repentance is where you talk to God and ask Him to forgive *all* your sins. It is also where you forgive your transgressors (those who have sinned against you). In many ways, this is also one of the hardest steps – especially when you feel you are right. Forgiveness is a continuous process.

"Then came Peter to Him and said, 'Lord, how oft shall my brother sin against me, and I forgive Him/ Jesus saith unto Him. Till seven times.' Jesus saith unto Him, 'I say not unto thee, until seven times: but, until seventy times seven."
– *Matthew 18:21-22.*

By forgiving yourself and others, you begin your process of releasing as you move into step 3.

Prayer is a very necessary component in the forgiveness step. When you pray, know that you are in the presence of God. What is prayer?

Prayer is simply talking to God in plain language. In many situations, we pray without being conscious of it. Sometimes we pray in desperation or during crisis. We may say, "Oh God help me! Lord have Mercy!" Whether your prayers are unconscious or intentional, God hears your prayers. Be patient for His answer.

".… The farmer waits for the precious crop from the earth, being patient with it until it receives the early and the late rains." – James 5:7

According to Jesuit Father John Fuch, Director at The Palisades Retreat and Faith Formation Center in Federal Way (Tacoma), "There is a difference between conscious prayer and unconscious prayer. He said it's impossible not to pray - talking about unconscious prayer saying that even babies know how to pray. He compared prayer with breathing saying that prayer is as necessary spiritually as breathing is physically." Fuch also said that, "Another description of prayer is noticing that God is trying to get our attention, and then letting God have our attention. God is signaling to us all the time and through everything. It is often helpful for people to go to a place that is beautiful, quiet, and conducive to prayer – where God can get their attention."[1]

"Hear my prayer, O LORD, and let my cry come unto thee. Hide not thy face from me in the day when I am in trouble; incline thine ear unto me: in the day when I call answer me speedily."
– Psalm 102:1-2

---

[1] Jesuit Father John Fuch, director at The Palisades Retreat and Faith Formation Center in Federal Way (Tacoma) you can express your desires, hopes, and dreams. When you ask God for forgiveness, something miraculous happens in your life. This is when true healing begins. No matter how large or small your sins, He will forgive you. It is not based on size or degree. Yes, *ALL SIN*, even if your sins are for lying, cheating, disrespecting or mentally hurting another human being, He will forgive you and others. Just ask! *"If you forgive anyone, I also forgive him. And what I have forgiven – if there was anything to forgive – I have forgiven in the sight of Christ for your sake."* – 2 Corinthians 2:10

I believe that prayer is necessary for us to live a meaningful life. All we need to do is simply tell God all about it. He knows it anyway. He encourages us to talk (pray) to Him. With Him,

[1] He is nonjudgmental. No chastisement. He has no discipline, punishment, rebuke, scolding or reprimand. He is God and God is love. He is compassionate.

"Therefore, I say unto you, what things so ever ye desire, when ye pray, believe that ye receive them, and ye shall have them. And when ye stand praying, forgive, if ye have ought against any: that your Father also which is in heaven may forgive you your trespasses. But if ye do not forgive, neither will your Father which is in heaven forgive your trespasses." – Mark 11:24-26.

Q & A
What does forgiveness mean to you?

Third Step of Faith: Releasing

"Then He said, 'Let me go, for the day is breaking' But Jacob said, 'I will not let you go, unless you bless me.'" – Genesis 32:26

What is releasing? According to the English Thesaurus (U.S) – releasing is letting go, freeing, discharging, liberating and letting loose. Simply put, it means to "Let go and let God."

Let us examine each meaning closely as it relates to faith:

Letting go – breaking the hold of fear, guilt, shame, pride, and embarrassment. You are letting go of tiredness, frustration and hopelessness, and then coming to God just as you are. Releasing it. *Free* – freedom, to be liberated, think, grow and dream. … *"and where the Spirit of the Lord is, there is freedom"* – *2 Corinthians 3:17 NIV.* Freedom to experience life to the fullest.

Freedom to experience the miraculous power of God. Releasing your fears is the key.

Discharge – emancipate, expulsion and eject negative thoughts. Releasing it.

Liberate – unshackling bondage. "*And I will walk at liberty for: I seek thy precepts*" – *Psalm 119:45 KJV.* Releasing it.

Let loose – untying or unraveling the chains of hurt. Releasing it.

Announcement – telling the world how good God is. Releasing it with your mouth and actions. Not doubting.

If you are faced with different challenges in life (job pressure, broken marriage, addiction, mental instability, unemployment, drugs, gambling, etc.), turn IT (intentional trial) back to GOD. Yes, God knows about it anyway, but want you to release IT over to Him.

As my sister Bertha summarized it: "God never brings you into a situation, the same way He brought you out."

Q & A
1. How do you define "releasing" in your life?
2. How do you release the pains or hurts of the past?
3. Do you truly believe that if you let it go to God (like Jacob did in Gen 32:26), that God will handle it, work all things for your good – and bless it? Discuss this.

Footstep Prayer: Heavenly Father, I thank You for guiding me to Release those things in my life that have held me hostage. Amen.

Mama's Pearl

part one

Born with little twigs of hair
Warm cocoa brown and cute
Zesty mannered and debonair
Soft as bamboo skin attribute

A smile to brighten the day
Five pounds one ounce
A bundle of joy
A treasure from God
Strength in mind and heart

She's Mama's Pearl
But God's Creation
Fresh as Spring Waters
Embracing sweet aspirations

Mama's reflection in the mirror
Providing unconditional love
Unlimited caring and sharing
Wisdom from God above

Strong and capable Special in many ways
Mama's Pearl but God's Creation
Give Me Love
Count My Blessings & Appreciation

Mama's Pearl

part two

"Your heart shall thrill and rejoice, because the abundance of the sea shall be brought to you."
—Isaiah 60:5

Few oyster shells have a pearl
Unique, distinct and one of a kind
Beauty to the eye of the beholder
Small true gem inside

An aquatic shell designed by God
The Creator with you in mind
In coastal waters it thrives
Rarer than a diamond and harder to find
It's small, it's strong
A true jewel to take
Like a flawless, colorless diamond
Perfect clarity and perfect weight

My heart thrills and rejoices
From this abundance of the sea
Not every oyster has a pearl
The Creator chooses the oysters it will be

Some empty shells will surface
Cause God has this pearl in His hands
He cares for it while His angels rejoice
Cause one heart and life expand

From the oceanic depths of the open sea

Like an angel it graces God's gallery
With intoxicating beauty making its mark
Like a divine treasure from God's heart

Part One and Part Two are dedicated to
my daughter Angela Coburn
Written by Margret V. Oglesby

Fourth Step of Faith: Trusting God

"Trust in the Lord with all thine heart; and lean not unto thine own understanding. In all thy ways acknowledge Him, and He shall direct thy paths. – Proverbs 3:5-6

When you put your trust totally in God, you are completely relying on Him, and you are confident that He will do exactly what He promised. What does it really mean to trust God completely? To trust God completely means belief, conviction, hope, dependence, confidence, and, yes, faith that He has the power to do all things (great or small). In Him, you have faith in the present, belief for a joyful tomorrow, and hope for a better future. When you put your trust totally in God, you believe in His Word boldly and with confidence. Through faith, you know that God has divine power to move mountains out of your path, to whisper transforming love to your situation, and show you favor through His grace. *"For by grace are ye saved through faith; and that not of yourselves: it is the gift of God …" – Ephesians 2:8.* What a gift it is! To have God's favor is the best gift you can have.

When they came to the crowd, a man approached Jesus and knelt before Him. "Lord, have mercy on my son," he said. "He has seizures and is suffering greatly. He often falls in the fire or into the water. I brought him to your disciples, but

*they could not heal him." "O unbelieving and perverse generation,"
Jesus replied, "how long shall I stay with you? How long shall I put
up with you? Bring the boy here to me." Jesus rebuked the demon,
and it came out of the boy, and he was healed from the moment.
Then the disciples came to Jesus in private and asked, "Why couldn't
we drive it out?" He replied, "Because you have so little faith. I
tell you the truth, if you have faith as small as a mustard seed, you
can say to this mountain, "Move from here to there," and it will
move. Nothing will be impossible for you." – Matthew 17:14-20*

*"For He says, in the time of my favor I heard you, and in the day of sal-
vation I helped you. I tell you, now is the time of God's favor, now is the
day of salvation." – 2 Corinthians 6:2*

God will provide you with all the desires of your heart. You will then
experience God's unconditional love. *"Delight thyself also in the Lord;
and He shall give thee the desires of thine heart." – Psalm 37:4 KJV.*
God's blessings are given to us freely. He has supernatural powers
beyond comprehension and logic. *"Jesus said unto him, if thou canst
believe, all things are possible to him that believeth." – Mark 9:23.
"Blessed is the man that trusteth in the Lord, and whose hope the Lord
is." – Jeremiah 17:7*

Q & A

1. Proverbs 3:5-6 says "Trust in the Lord with _and___. In
   all thy ways _____ and_____."
2. Why is it impossible to please God without faith?
3. What does it mean to trust God completely?
4. What did 2 Corinthians 6:2 say about God's favor?
5. If you delight yourself in the Lord, what did God promise?

Footstep Prayer:
I trust and thank You, Abba (Father) that You have given me divine
favor and have always kept your promises. Amen.

She Walks...

Wilma Lambert-Oglesby

With poise, self-assurance, and elegance; Classy, Strong and Inspired with Confidence. Head lifted with grace, beauty, and dignity; Accomplished excellence and integrity

She Smiles...
With character, kindness, patience and gentleness; Blossomed flower with exuberance exquisiteness; Empowered blessings projected to many; Her heart opened to *"El Shaddai"* God of plenty

She Speaks...
With self-confidence, enthusiasm, and splendor; She gives words of encouragement and excitement for life that soar; Uplifting expres-

sions like a morning latte; Flavored freshness like the warmth of the Sunray

She Works…
With definitive achievement and devotion Excels with purpose beyond expectation Shines in darkness and sparkles in light Anticipated job well done with insight

Because She Walks for
Christ the King…

Loved, respected, and appreciated with tremendous purpose articulated
Superb legacy of life's journey awaits
Woman of sincerity with sustained faith

Written by Margret V. Oglesby Dedicated to Wilma Oglesby-Lambert and Bertha Oglesby-Stanley (my sisters) and Augustine Outtz (my friend)

Fifth Step of Faith: Transformation

"Do not conform any longer to the pattern of this world but be transformed by the renewing of your mind. Then you will be able to test and approve what God's will is – His good, pleasing, and perfect will." – Roman 12:2 NIV

This step takes you on an amazing journey as you discover God like never before. This is when God is revealing His divine and anointing power in your life. In this step of transformation, you are becoming the person that God meant you to be in mind, body and spirit (the soul). You begin to change and transform your lifestyle and even your views on existence. You become <u>new</u> in Christ. The <u>old</u> you is gone. His miraculous power transforms you to an enriched outcome. As we see the changing seasons, we, too, will change. Change is inevitable. It is also certain, expected and to be anticipated. In fact, it is a natural part of life. Within every ending is also a new beginning. As one door closes, another door opens. However, it is so hard for most people to come to grips with change. That is why we must step out on faith and be excited about God and life because change is unavoidable. His miraculous power transforms you to an enriched outcome. Your faith in God has transformed your life. Being transformed, you have liberated yourself from the strongholds of the past. This is good news and a great place to be in faith. You feel good about yourself and others. You celebrate life because it is a constant revival of renewing your mind. God has performed a miracle in you. *"To be made new in the attitude of your minds; and to put on the new self, created to be like God in true righteousness and holiness." – Ephesians 4 23-24.*

When you are transformed, you become <u>new</u> in Christ. You are changed from the inside out. Can you visualize being changed from the inside out? You are recreated in mind, body, and spirit. Your views change. Your thinking changes. Your mannerism changes. Your talk changes. And your daily walk changes. *"Therefore, if anyone is in Christ, he is a new creation; the old has gone, the new has come!" – 2 Corinthians 5:17.*

Why is this? Because God is in you and you in God. When you are transformed, you are changed physically, mentally and emotionally. When you put your faith in God, you know that He will never change. *"Jesus Christ is the same yesterday and today and forever." –Hebrew 13:8*

Q & A
1. How has God transformed your life?
2. Do you believe in God's miraculous powers today?

Footstep Prayer: Heavenly Father, I know that only by Your Amazing Grace and Mercy, I am transformed to do Your will and for Your purpose. Amen.

Thomas Girls

Trinita (Shelle), Thomas and Brusha

Veessa Oglesby

God's Butterfly

In the beginning, God created the universe
Then He spoke all species and animal life to birth
Both large and small, that moved by land
And those that mounted with
great wings as eagles can
Some transformed from small like the butterfly
That emerged and filled God's beautiful sky
For this, we give thanks....

He then created in His image the man
And from man's rib God created woman
Since the beginning of time woman soared high
As gracious with purpose like the butterfly
From her beauty and transformed energy
She became like God's butterfly and was free
For this, we give thanks....

She nurtured in the beginning of motherhood
Giving tender-care to her young
to flourish as they should

God covers mothers with His wings
Giving direction and power to her dreams
He deepens her desire to encourage and love
Like the butterfly and like the dove
For you, we give thanks....

God gives wisdom freely as the rain
Like a butterfly transcends and embrace change
She goes beyond limits as she grows in her faith
Like God's butterfly, she is given His grace
For you, we give thanks....

Mothers are the fiber that holds the family
together – you rock!
Landscaped with various colors, shapes and sizes
– no limit box!
As butterflies' descent on objects to bless it
God will ALWAYS keep his promises
For this, we give thanks....

Inspiration consumes you to make a
difference on every hand
Your life is one of purpose
according to God's plan
With God the Father, God the Christ

Like the butterfly you live a transformed life
You encourage all to dream BIG and pray
Celebrate and appreciate Mothers – EVERYDAY!
To God, we give thanks....

Written by
Margret V. Oglesby
Dedicated to all mothers both past and present
(Especially to my Mama, Veessa Oglesby)

Sixth Step of Faith: Praising God

*"Let everything that hath breath praise the Lord. Praise ye
the Lord." – Psalms 150:6. "Praise ye the Lord. Praise ye
the Lord from the heavens: praise Him in the heights. Praise
ye Him, all his angels: praise ye Him, all his hosts."
– Psalms 148:1-2.*

To praise means to worship, glorify, adore, honor, give thanks and devotion to God.

PRAISE IS REAL WORSHIP. *"God is spirit, and those who worship Him must worship in spirit and truth" – John 4:24.* When you praise God, you are telling Him how much you love Him; you glorify Him and magnify His holy name. You don't even need a reason to praise Him. You praise Him for who He is – the Almighty omnipotent God. You also praise God for the victory over all circumstances. Halleluiah is the highest praise. *"Every day will I bless thee; and I will praise thy name forever and ever. Great is the Lord, and greatly to be praised; and his greatness is unsearchable." – Psalms 145:2-3. Praise ye the Lord. Praise the Lord, O my soul. While I live will I praise the Lord: I will sing praises unto my God while I have any being." – Psalms 146:1-2.*

Praising God with gratitude… I like to think of this as praising God with a great attitude. Gratitude = great-attitude.

As Byron Cage says, "praise Him in the morning, praise Him at noonday and praise Him when the sun goes down." This is real-time praise 24/7. *"Praise ye the Lord. Sing unto the Lord a new song, and his praise in the congregation of saints." – Psalms 140:1.* Songstress Benita Jones says it this way: "I love You, I love You, I love You, Lord, today, because You care for me in such a special way. That's why I praise You, I lift You up and I magnify Your name. That is why my heart is filled with praise. My heart, my mind, my soul belongs to You, because You paid the price way back on Calvary. That is why I praise You, I lift You up and I magnify Your name. That is why my heart is filled with praise." *"Let us always offer to God our sacrifice of Praise." - Hebrews 13:15.* Thank God (Dieu Merci)!

From the New Church Hymnal Doxology by
Thomas Ken & Louis Bourgeois:
Praise God from whom all blessing flow, Praise Him all creatures here below. Praise Him above ye heavenly host. Praise Father, Son and Holy Ghost. Amen.

"And whatever you do, in word or deed, do everything in the name of the Lord Jesus, giving thanks to God the Father through Him." – Colossians 3:17

"O God, thou art my God; <u>early will I seek thee</u>: <u>my soul thirsteth for thee</u> …"– Psalms 63:1 "Because thou hast been my help, therefore in the <u>shadow of thy wings will I rejoice</u>" –Psalms 63:7

Q & A
1. What happens when you praise God? *Read Psalms 146-151 David's Psalms of Praise*
2. Discuss the association between praise and prayer?
3. What does it mean *"when praises go up, blessings come down?"*

Footstep Prayer:
Heavenly Father, I praise Your Holy Name. No other Name is worthy to be praised. Amen.

Power of Praise

Come and take refuge
Within God's sanctuary of praise
Manifestation of the Holy Spirit
God's power and protective rays

Only God Almighty gives power
By His colossal spoken Word
He created the world and its firmaments
The King of Kings and Lord of Lords

God created man in His own image
And God saw that it was good
The man in the mirror is mankind
He clothes with love and provides food

Envision the energy "*The Son*" produces
He defends and protects from above
Oh' be thirsty for His power and drink
From the cup of His divine love

Within God's sanctuary take shelter
The head of all principalities and power
Take on the whole armor of God
Don't wait a second, minute or hour

God gives power within His sanctuary
Great and mighty things to teach
Faith and prayer are the tools
Love is the power key to preach

No one can separate from the love of God
With God's unconditional grace you will stand

Nor height, nor depth, nor any creature
Only God has all power in His hands

Written by Margret V. Oglesby
Dedicated to Pastor Dallas Powell
Sanctuary of Praise Church

Seventh Step of Faith: Keeping the Faith

*"Know therefore that the Lord thy God, He is God, the faithful
God, which keepeth covenant and mercy with them that love
Him and keep his commandments to a thousand generations."*
– Deuteronomy 7:9

*"For by grace are ye saved through faith; and
that not of yourselves:
It is the gift of God." – Ephesians 2:8*

Keeping the Faith is a lifetime journey with God. He will show you favor and bring the right people in your life, at the right time, and in the right season. His divine order will direct your life. You have unlimited potential and opportunities. His love, wisdom, kindness, and peace will forever guide your life. He will show you favor in so many ways. Your mind cannot perceive the goodness of God's grace. The more you love Him, the more He loves you. The more you give Him, the more He gives to you – and allows you to be a blessing to others. He wants you to be a recipient of His blessings and a giver to others.

"And God is able to provide you with every blessing in abundance, so that by always having enough of everything, you may share abundantly in every good work." – 2 Corinthians 9:8

Keeping the Faith, you will <u>continuously</u> receive all the blessings and wonderful things God has for you. This is something to really SHOUT about! Keeping and maintaining the relationship with God is powerful and the most fulfilling of all the steps. This is where God keeps His promises to always be with you.

"...Yea, I have spoken it, I will also bring it to pass; I have purposed it, I will also do it." – Isaiah 46:11. "My covenant will I not break, nor alter the thing that is gone out of my lips." – Psalm 89:34.

In this step, you have an intimate passion for God's love that goes beyond human understanding. You have the anointing power of the Holy Spirit in every step of your life. Your actions speak louder than words because God's Spirit is all over you and through you – in your walk, in your talk, and in the very air that you breathe.

"Her ways are ways of pleasantness, and all her paths are peace." – Proverbs 3:17 KJV

"Then shall thou walk in thy way safely, and thy foot shall not stumble." Proverbs 3:23 KJV

God's blessings are overflowing. You are truly stepping out on faith in your daily walk with God. Remember the poem 'Footprints.' This poem sums it up. He is always with us in the good and bad times.

By Faith

– Hebrews 11

Now faith is being sure of what we hope for and certain of what we do not see. This is what the ancients were commended for.

> ➤ By faith we understand that the universe was formed at God's command, so that what is seen was not made out of what was visible.

- By faith Enoch was taken from this life, so that he did not experience death; he could not be found, because God had taken him away. For before he was taken, he was commended as one who pleased God. And without faith it is impossible to please God, because anyone who comes to Him must believe that He exists and that He rewards those who earnestly seek Him.
- By faith Abraham, when called to go to a place he would later receive as his inheritance, obeyed and went, even though he did not know where he was going. By faith, he made his home in the Promised Land like a stranger in a foreign country; he lived in tents, as did Isaac and Jacob, who were heirs with him of the same promise. For he was looking forward to the city with foundations, whose architect and builder is God.
- By faith Abraham, even though he was past age (and Sarah herself was barren) was able to become a father because he considered him faithful. And so, from this one man, and he as good as dead, came descendants as numerous as the stars in the sky and as countless as the sand of the seashore.
- All these people were still living by faith when they died. They did not receive the things promised; they only saw them and welcomed them from a distance... Instead, they were longing for a better country – a heavenly one. Therefore, God is not ashamed to be called their God for He has prepared a city for them.
- By faith Abraham, when God tested him, offered Isaac as a sacrifice, He who had received the promises was about to sacrifice his one and only son even though God had said to him, "it is through Isaac that your offspring will be reckoned." Abraham reasoned that God could raise the dead, and figuratively speaking, he did receive Isaac back from death.
- By faith Isaac blessed Jacob and Esau in regard to their future.

- By faith Jacob, when he was dying, blessed each of Joseph's sons and worshipped as he leaned on the top of his staff.
- By faith Joseph, when his end was near, spoke about the exodus of the Israelites from Egypt and gave instructions about his bones.
- By faith Moses' parents hid him for three months after he was born because they saw he was no ordinary child and they were not afraid of the king's edict.
- By faith Moses, when he had grown up, refused to be known as the son of Pharaoh's daughter. He chose to be mistreated along with the people of God rather than to enjoy the pleasures of sin for a short time. He regarded disgrace for the sake of Christ as of greater value that the treasures of Egypt because he was looking ahead to his reward. By faith, he left Egypt, not fearing the king's anger; he persevered because he saw him who is invisible. By faith he kept the Passover and sprinkling of blood so that the destroyer of the first born would not touch the first born of Israel.
- By faith the people passed through the
- Red Sea as on dry land, but when the Egyptians tried to do so, they were drowned.
- By faith the walls of Jericho fell, after the people had marched around them for seven days
- By faith the prostitute Rehab, because she welcomed the spies, was not killed with those who were disobedient.

These were all commended for their faith, yet none of them received what had been promised. God had planned something better for us so that only together with us would they be made perfect. – Hebrews 11:39

As Jesuit Father John Fuch puts it, "*I think God spoils us in order to entice us, and then God helps us walk on our own, like a child learning to walk, so that we can grow in faith. When we experience consolation, in some way there's no need for faith because it's self-evident. It's a time of light and clarity. But when we're in desolation it's a time of darkness and blindness. But that's when we have to practice faith and trust that God is there, even though we don't feel God's presence.*[22]

---

[2] Jesuit Father John Fuch, director at The Palisades Retreat and Faith Formation Center in Federal Way (Tacoma)

Queen Margret and King Bill

All the King's Men

All the King's men; black men, young and old
Embraced by the armor of faith as the Bible
foretold. Men with insight, maturity, and
hindsight; Inspired with remarkable foresight.

Not just black men as providers and protectors
But men as fathers, leaders and correctors
Christian men providing a positive bond of
manhood, but overcome by love and strong brotherhood

You're our hero with peaceful strength
Honorable men with strong confidence
Wise men who educate and reciprocate love
Anointed by the omnipotent God from above

Innovative men with deep perception and
observation. Loyal and honest men highly
motivated. Men to encourage other black men
Inspirational men and great friends

Created in God's image like no other
Godly men worshipping as brothers
Men of virtue and men of honor
Solidarity is your true color

Faithful and thoughtful men is your legacy
Who study God's Word with intensity
Always willing to give a helping hand
Reaching out to your fellow man

Often, we fail to give your due crown
Yet we recognize your faithfulness is profound
Respected greatly through your ministry
Victorious journey is your destiny

All the King's disciples and all the King's men
We are so grateful to you time and time again
Hallelujah to the sovereign God we sing
You are Christ the King!

Written by Margret V. Oglesby
Dedicated to The King's Men at CTK
and William H. Anderson Jr

King and Queen

PART TWO

The Power of Faith

"The power at work with us is able to accomplish abundantly far more than all we can ask or imagine." – Ephesians 3:20

"Then He touched their eyes and said, "according
to your faith let it be done to you."
Matthew 9:29

Do you know that each day you live in faith, you have miraculous power – beyond imagination? God said it and it is true. You have His invincible faith.

"And Jesus answering saith unto them, Have faith in God. For verily I say unto you, that whosoever shall say unto this mountain, be thou removed, and be thou cast into the sea; and shall not doubt in his heart but shall believe that those things which He saith shall come to pass; He shall have whatsoever He saith."
Mark 11:22-23

Invincible Faith

IF is unshakable

IF is unbeatable

IF is unwavering

IF is God's truth

IF is constant

IF is to trust God

"According to Invincible Faith in God, "...it is evident that Christ Jesus placed the utmost importance of one's having faith in the almightiness of God. Those who came to him to be healed were made whole according to their faith. It was not a blind faith which impelled them. Rather, in seeking God for divine help, they opened their consciousness to the ministration of the Christ, the true idea of God, which Jesus imparted to them.[3]"

---

[3] Fred W. Decker from April 8, 1967 issue of the Christian Science Sentinel –
    Dedicated to Brusha Lambert

PART THREE

Poetry for the Soul

Several generations are born with a poetic heart. I am so grateful for this special gift of love. Thank You God.

Mama's Love

Mama, I thank you for your love – although I have caused you many tears. Mama, you continued to love me through all your graying years.

Mama, you forgave my undeserving soul within. Mama, you said "let it go" – so God's healing could begin.

Mama, you often prayed for me when my plans fell through. Mama, you said, "don't worry baby, *God got you!*" Mama, through all my challenges you held my hand. Embraced and encouraged me – giving me the strength *to stand.*"

Mama, you have always fostered compassion and forgiveness. Mama, you have filled my life with spiritual fullness. Mama, I know you have made great sacrifices for me. But through God's grace, I gave back my life to Thee.

Mama, you are so nurturing, loving and strong. Mama, you are highly blessed by God alone. Mama, you said that love grows greater as it is given away. And not to let the enemy cause me to stray!

Mama, you taught me that love is reflected through God's eyes. Mama, I've learned God is good and we're blessed to be wise. Mama, I may not have walked your desired path. But I thank God for allowing me to travel the road I tread.

My roadmap of life is centered in God's full trend. His love continues and never ends… Mama, when I look at me *NOW - I SEE YOU!* – a Mama who has become a beacon light, humble and true.

Mama, I am kind, warm-hearted and free – because of the Mama, you have taught me to be. Without a doubt God's love is the base so, celebrate that all mamas are wondrously made.

Written by Margret V. Oglesby
Dedicated to my Mama, Veessa Oglesby
Christ the King United Church of Christ
Mother's Day –May 13, 2012

Mama's Wisdom

Borne Kissed by God
Wisdom that none compare
With long Silvery Hair
Complexion smooth and fair

Seven children are her glory
Faith was her sword & shield
Rooted & planted good seeds
Producing a fruitful field

Proud mother and grandmother
She disciplined none with anger
Paving and preparing the pathway
Guiding us to avoid danger

Life was not always easy
Sometimes she shed some tears
But blessed with faith & unwavering love
All her seventy-five years

All things she handled with care
God only knows how much she had to bear
With enduring spiritual vitality

She ministered to the sick and elderly

My mentor, gifted and wise
Many things seen through her eyes
So…blessed to see her children grow
Allowing God's Power to flow

Putting trust always in God
She prayed everyday
God bless & protect my children
As they travel life's highway
Her words spoken with Spiritual Power
Surrendering to God the High Tower

Life will have some ups & downs
But God has *already* anointed a crown
Before you were born your destiny was defined
To this special place in time

God created Mothers to birth us here
No worry. No ignorance. No fear.
All to God's Amazing Grace we pray
With gratitude we *Celebrate* Mother's Day!

Author Margret V. Oglesby
Dedicated to Mama Veessa Oglesby

A Woman's Touch

When your life is touched by a woman
who is engineered to love;
Even from the beginning of time
God's blessings flow from above.

There are times when only a
woman's touch
Can understand our tears,
Can soothe our disappointments
And calm all our fears.

There are times when only a
woman's love
Can share the joy we feel
When something once dreamed about
Quite suddenly becomes real.

There are times when only a
woman's faith
Can guide us on life's way
And instill in us the confidence
We need from day to day.

With a women's caring heart and a hug
with a pat on your back she will say. "Baby
treat all with kindness and respect because
you will never know who you'll need next, but
be positive and encouraged with NO regrets.

A woman's touch is *like a star*
That illuminates the night
Like the soul's guiding light.

A woman's strength is *like an anchor*
In life's stormy seas; It was in the beginning
of time, it is now and forever to the end
Not just a woman, but a friend!

Written by Margret V. Oglesby
in honor of Women's Day CTK,

Dedicated to my sisters: Joetta Powell, Mary Gordon,
Wilma Lambert, and Bertha Stanley

Was I Dreaming?

About Marriage

Was I dreaming when you said you loved me
As we exchanged wedding vows?
Was I dreaming as he said 'til death do us part
As we shared years from the heart?

Was I dreaming as you gave your heart away
And I was left only with my dreams?
Was I dreaming when we said goodbye
Moving to a new life as friends?

Was I dreaming when we bought our first home
Vowing to not be left alone?
Was I dreaming as we travelled to distant lands
Breathing in nature and walking hand in hand?

Was I dreaming when we met new friends
Solemnly declaring never to be lonely again?
Was I dreaming as God took my hand
to lead and guide me on the right path?

As I reflected and held tight to my dreams
Suddenly truth and reality were redeemed
With little faith, I let go and let God above
Gently give me His unconditional love.

Written by Margret V. Oglesby
My Reflections

Greener Grass

Some folks take a different path because
the grass seems greener on the other side
Not knowing they are already rooted
in the soil that is planted deep and wide.

The greener grass is how life appears from
the opposite side of a paradigm
while you are not focused on what
you already have at the time.

So, change how you see things from the
mind-eye and focus your insight on God from on high.
Whatever road or path you trod
Remember all reflects to God.

Written by Margret V. Oglesby
My Reflections
May-2018

Sunray

Marvelous the beauty of the sunray
that reflects upon the earth
Oh, how I love the morning sunrise
like a renaissance birth!
A sun kiss received from God
performing His daily duty
I tune out the noise of the world and
witness its beauty

How excellent are the prayers sent today?
That my sunray will witness this beauty I pray
As our eyes behold the magnificent
wonders of nature
Awaken winged angels (birds) as
they sing praises to our Creator
Within God's sky I visualize and
witness His sunlight
Like no others creation from God
known by day or night

Created just for me He designed this sunray
Oh, how grateful I am for this day
In and out of season, He let the sun rise above
He proved His love by giving
His unconditionally love

God chose for me to know His name
Oh, how thankful to God – I proclaim!
As I envisioned the warmth of his grace
I imagined his loving embrace

I close my eyes to feel my heartbeat
I synchronize in tune as each beat completes
I marvel at how the earth needs water to flow
Nourish sunflowers that reflects beauty and grow

I marveled at how the sunray kisses
the earth to feed His babe
As unique as the rainbow comes in
many colors and many shades

Daily talks are refreshing and deep
As drowsiness come upon my brow
before I said goodnight for sleep
Words of love and encouragement flows
as sweet as the honeycomb
And as high as the eagle soar when it roams

You are my sunshine and my sunray
I appreciate and love God everyday!

Written in 2010 by Margret V. Oglesby
Reflecting God's Love

Do You Remember?

Do you remember when we first talked and
how we communicated for hours?
How we listened to each other's heartbeat and
how we shared intimacy with only word power?

Do you remember how we exchanged life stories
and how we prayed that we would like each other
and how we visualized each other's beauty in the
mind-eye?

Do you remember how we discussed the living
Word of God and how the Word has POWER
and that God shows us the beauty of every
flower?

Do you remember when we first met and you
gave me a gold rose and I gave you a birthday
teddy bear to hold?

Do you remember our first embrace of a hug and
kiss and how we laughed singing silly songs and
not being the first to say goodnight to dismiss?

Do you remember that we did not hear the bells
ring and did not feel the anticipated magnetic
intensity that we hoped and trusted would have a
love connection? Although our spirit connected
from a distance, God knows what is best for us.

When did it end or did it ever begin?
Was it a relationship or just a friendship shared
from a distance? or did it motivate only from my

selfish persistence?

Did I only visualize a romantic encounter
or was I simply in love with the thought of a new
friend? God answered me and said, "it's time to
let it go and let God handle this so your healing can begin."

Written by Margret V. Oglesby
Dedicated to a distant friend

Anointed Hands

Minister of Music
at Christ the King
Giving encouragement
as we sing
You inspire us to
worship and praise
Pouring into us hope
in every phase

You are spiritually
gifted
As God is uplifted
You are faithful and blessed
Your anointed hands give God access

Choir rehearsals with transformed energy
As your extraordinary smile sparkles dignity
God speaks through the chords of your
melody as you proclaim His victory

Your anointing is where miracles are
As you go beyond limits by far
You provide us the right music mix
Giving God the glory – the right fix

A brilliant musician and singer with
passionate heat – with sounds of melody as
you play and sing to the beat; producing
harmonious compositions in unity – as you
belt out songs that harvest continuity

Guiding and teaching us new songs

Inspiring instructions that are life-long
You go beyond the black and white key
Being all that God anointed you to be

Written by Margret V. Oglesby Dedicated to
Shamar Jordan, Minister of Music
Christ the King United Church of Christ

You are the Man

Happy Father's Day!

Today, we are celebrating fathers and fatherhood.
Not just fathers, but all brotherhood.
We are observing men that motivate
and inspire with positive length!
We thank God for your paternal bond
that gives us strength!

YOU ARE THE MAN!

Yes, you are the man who mentors with strong confidence –
With encouraging words that guide and represent.
Some may say you have a difficult time expressing your best,
Yet, you will work long hours for us from sunrise to sunset!

YOU ARE THE MAN!

You are the heart and soul lesson; you
influence our lives and are a blessing!
I thank God for my daddy so much –
For teaching us the value and VIRTUE of hard work!

YOU ARE THE MAN!

You engage many by being an example
of love –You are truly a blessing sent from heaven above!

Thank you for being our big brother, not
just our friend; We love you! You are
God's warriors to the very end!

The greatest gift of a father's love
was God sacrificing his only son through the blood.

GOD IS THE MAN!
Written by Margret V. Oglesby Dedicated
to my Daddy, Joe Nathan Oglesby
and to my two wonderful brothers,
E. Hammond Oglesby and White Oglesby
Recited at Christ the King UCC
Church for Father's Day 06/21/2015

Man of Integrity

Nathan Williams, you are honored today as a man of integrity by your Queen, Reita Williams, family and friends. You are indeed a man of honor and loyalty. Gifted by God and crowned with royalty.

You are reliable and dependable. As surely as the sun and moon, you rise with dignity and integrity. You have a caring persona that precedes your education, skills and work ethics as if you're part of a three- dimensional virtual reality.

What is a man of integrity? A man of integrity seeks words of wisdom like gold and tells the stories untold. Yet, is an incredibly good listener as he hears the cries from the young and old.

What is a man of integrity? A man of integrity connects with God in prayer every day to rejuvenate and replenish his mental and emotional soul's energy. For there is no better spiritual gift before starting each journey.

What is a man of integrity? A man of integrity surrounds himself with positive people and is not paralyzed or held hostage by others' opinions of him, but walks by faith and saved by God's amazing grace.

Who is this man of integrity? Nathan Williams, you are this man who does not compromise your integrity by what others say in unity. God has anointed you a deacon at Christ the King in solidarity with other deacons not about popularity, but divinity. You are a man who knows Jehovah Jireh will provide – Word amplified!

When God created your DNA, He knew you before you were born while yet in your mother's womb to sing with tenor harmonizing melodies in praise to His tune.

God has blessed you, Nathan, to celebrate seventy years as a son, a brother, a husband, a father and a friend. Not broken down by disappointing circumstances or occasional aches, yet you rise strong and strengthened by each step you take.

Whether you have climbed mountains to reach your destiny or have gone to the lowest crater for your untouched diamond, your like is controlled by God's grace as His faithful stipend. You have a big heart and only God knows your every desire, every vision and every dream. He alone created you to be Reita's king.

Written by Margret V. Oglesby and dedicated to
Deacon Nathan Williams

Bright Star

Bright star twinkling in the night Shining bright like
a diamond in the sky God could have chosen any star
for light This STAR witnessed the birth of Christ

Remembering that bright star
as the wise men travelled from afar To see baby Jesus born
in a manger Chosen to be our Lord and Savior.

Shining bright in the night Illuminating by glazing
light. From all the stars – it stood alone
As the light came to where Jesus was born

*".... And behold, the star that they had seen when it rose went
before them until it came to rest over the place where the child was.
When they saw the star, they rejoiced exceedingly with great joy."
– Matt 2:9-10*

The finest of garments God could have chosen when
He wrapped baby Jesus in swaddling clothes
Prepare the way of the Lord Jesus is the light of the world!

Like supermassive quasar-galactic radar Jesus is the super star

*".... For we have seen his star in the east and are come to worship Him."
– Matt 2:2*

What a star!

Written by Margret V. Oglesby Christmas 2015

A Woman's Touch

When your life is touched by a woman
Who is engineered to love;
Even from the beginning of time
God's blessings flow from above.

There are times when only a *woman's touch*
Can understand our tears,
Can soothe our disappointments
And calm all our fears.

There are times when only a *woman's love*
Can share the joy we feel
When something once dreamed about

Quite suddenly becomes real.

There are times when only a *woman's faith*
Can guide us on life's way
And instill in us the confidence
We need from day to day.
With a woman's caring heart and a hug
with a pat on your back
She'll speak. "Baby treat All with kindness
and respect Cause' you'll never know
who you'll need next
Be positive and encouraged with NO regrets.

A women's touch is *like a star*
That illuminates the night
Like the soul's guiding light.

A woman's strength is *like an anchor*
In life's stormy seas.
It was in the beginning of time, it is now and forever to the end
Not just a woman, but a friend!

Written by Margret V. Oglesby
Women's Day CTK, September 17, 2017
Dedicated to my sisters: Joetta Powell, Mary
Gordon, Wilma Lambert, and Bertha Stanley

Is Same God

Is same God
Who changed water to wine
Same miraculous God

Is same God
Who parted the Red Sea
Same awesome God

Is same God
Who healed the sick and raised the dead
Same healing God

Is same God
Who protected Daniel in the Lion's Den
Same saving God

Chorus:
When trouble comes your way
Don't give up!
When life knocks you down
Don't give up!
God is the same yesterday, today and forever
God will deliver you through your circumstances
So, don't give up!

A song written by Margret V. Oglesby
for Christ the King UCC Choir 10/1/2017

Nappy Hair

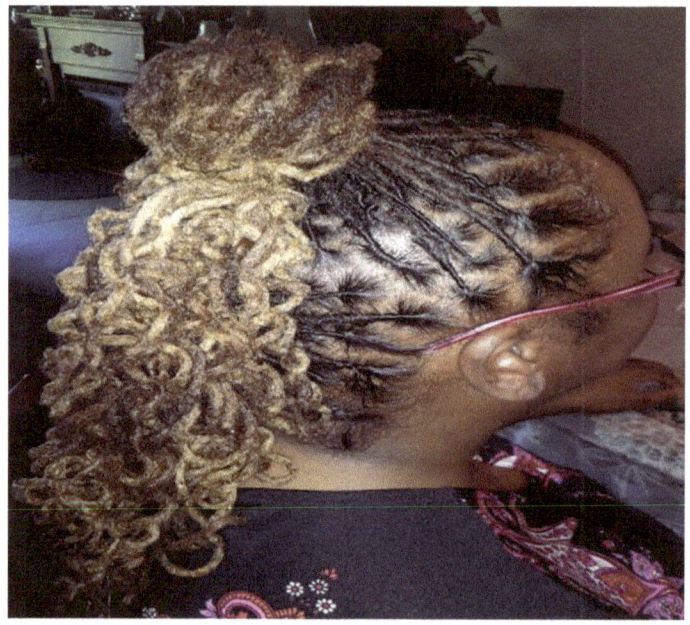

Nappy hair is good hair
Afrocentric hair
Dred-locked hair
Symmetric-braided hair
Corn-braided hair
Curled hair
Dyed hair

Roped hair
Pressed hair
Straight hair
Twigs
Mane hair
Straight hair
Natural hair
ALL GOOD HAIR!

Written by Margret V. Oglesby

PART FOUR

Traveling with God

Various journeys with William H. Anderson Jr.

Bill & Margret

Love can find itself in many places. I found love
in *Foley Missouri* on January 10, 2020.

I can honestly tell you "I found the man of my dreams."

My journey began swiftly with Bill Anderson following a church
gathering in Troy Missouri. This was when he told me that he
loved to travel. In fact, now I know that traveling is in his DNA.

After working 22 years at an industrial corporation and
an additional 14 years at a financial institution in St
Louis County, I decided to retire (June, 2020).

Margret's Retirement Day

After a full retirement, Bill said to me
"now we can really travel together." For our first travel
adventure, we flew into **Texas Airport**, **then drove to
Bozeman Montana, Pray Montana, Baker City,
Oregon, Oak Grove Oregon, then to Idaho, and on to Portland
Oregon**. Each city and state had its own special adventure for us.

Then in July 2021, we flew into **Fort Lauderdale** Florida
where we started our next journey driving to **Miami**,
Florida Keys & Key West.
So amazing & exciting!

As we began to travel more, God whispered to me to always
travel daily with God. This was when I corned the phrase **"Travel
with God"** from the shortest distance to the longest journey. We
started saying this to anyone and everyone coming or leaving
our presence. This became a strong affirmation of our faith.

Written by Margret V. Oglesby Dedicated
to William Hughes Anderson Jr
The Love of my Life

St Louis Gateway Arch

ST Louis Welcome Center

Union Station has over 8 million Travelers with various attractions, food and amenities. Explore the aquarium, rope course, Carousel and of course the St Louis Wheel

Margret, Wilma and Bertha Alton IL Train Station

Alton Illinois is also the Home of the Gentle Giant

Robert Wadlow bronze statue stands in Alton Illinois – known as the World's tallest man. He was said to be shy, friendly and very respectable.

O'Fallon MO

Angela (daughter) with Mary and Bertha (my sisters)

The Oglesby Family

A scene from the Past

Wilma is showing her grand-kids how to pick cotton as she
went down memory lane from many years ago in Arkansas.
NOT A FUN MEMORY – INFACT IT WAS
EXTREMELY HARD WORK from sun-up to sun-down. To
pick the cotton from the bolls, one had to simply grasp the cotton
ball at the base and twist it out while often cutting your finger.

Sgt. William Hughes Anderson Jr.

United States Air Force

Thank you for your Service

Well done, my good and faithful servant! – Matt 25:23

*Sgt Anderson is recognized on a flagpole in **Lebanon Illinois** in honor of serving six years in the United States Air Force. So proud and thank you for his service!*

*Bill is being honored by his son Allen in **Columbia MO** for his Military Service in The United States Air Force*

Salute to Excellence in Elsberry MO at Post 9064 VFW.
Honoring all Veterans who served in our military

VFW Post 9064

*Sgt Bill and Margret with Commander Bruce Watson and Liz
(VFW at Post 9064 Elsberry MO). This picture was taken at
the National Veteran Conference in **Kansas City** MO (2022)*

VFW Post 9064

Bill and Roger Macom served as Color Guard at Post 9064

Presenting the Colors is a military tradition dating back to the beginning of our country. The Rifle or Saber guards generally provides a ceremonial guard for each of the flags, this is a representation that they are safe and protected.

VVA Post 458 for Honor Flight as Color Guard
at Lambert International Airport

President and Commander Leonard Berkel

Post 458

Bill with Gene Vaucher doing Color Guard for Post 458 at Lambert International Airport

Bill with Bob Beiser doing Color Guard for Post 458 at Lambert Intl Airport

Bill in State Representative Office

Bill in Gov Eric Greitens office Jefferson City MO

*Accepting Resolution Award from the
Missouri House of Representative*

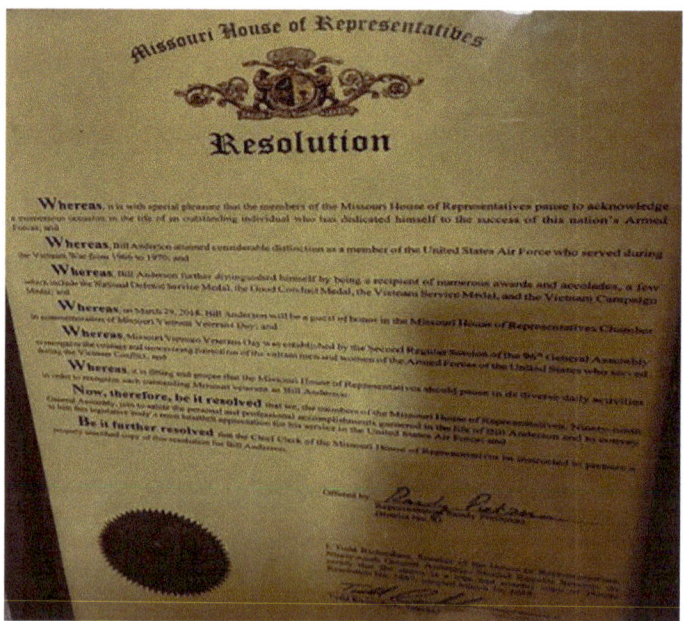

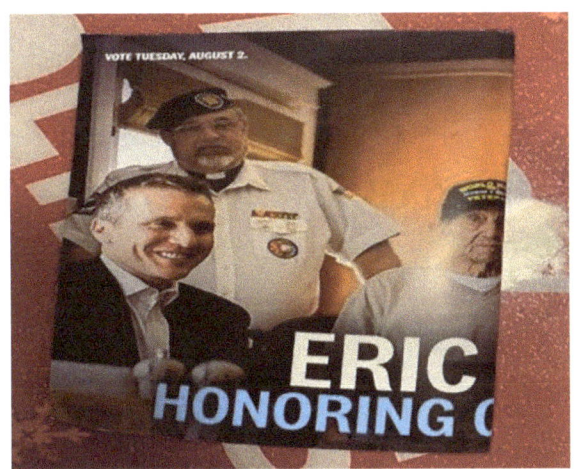

Bill with Bob Blake and Gov Eric
Greitens in Jefferson City MO

POW Ceremony O'Fallon MO

American Legion

Post 94 in Troy MO

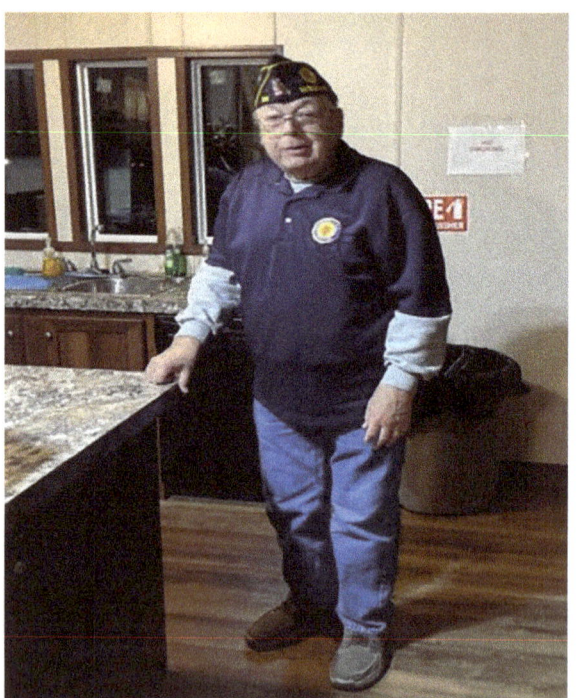

Commander Patrick McLaughlin

Remembering all veterans who served in our military both men and women

Thank you for your Service!

This is where it all started...

The Anderson Family

William & Odell Anderson
Together at Last 1991

Traveling with God is also dedicated to William and Odell Anderson
(Bill's Parents)

Celebrate Parents 50th Wedding Anniversary

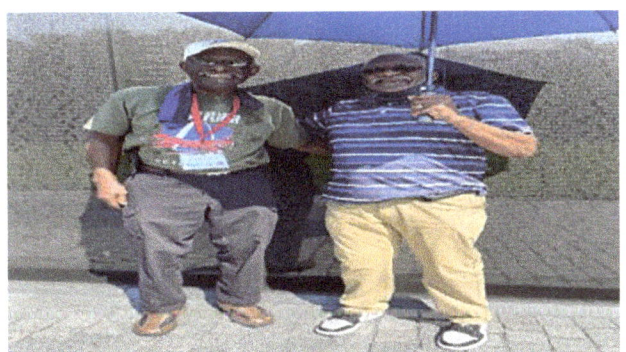

Vietnam Veteran Memorial

Honor Flight in Washington DC - Bill with Amber Cole, Kyle and Leon Anderson and Celeste

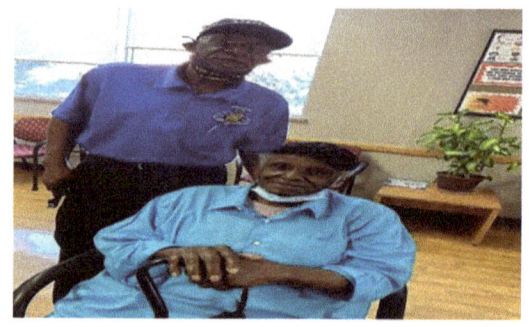

Bill's Brother George) now lives in Houston Texas.
He completes the seven steps of Faith

Bill and Leon visit parents' gravesite in Troy MO

Celebration with Anderson Family

Bill's Children and Grandchildren

Grand Children: Ro'Shawn and Michael with Sandra

Bill's Girls: Sandra, Celeste & D'era

Chicago Travels

Bill & Gloria

There is nothing like a brother and sister Smile
That carries love in the air for miles That lands like a butterfly
That gracefully travels high in the sky Love
is You and Me consistence
My sister, My friend from a distance

Mayme Metcalf

Honoring Mayme Metcalf born January 30, 1935 in St Louis, MO. She is Bill Anderson's first cousin and is the proud parent of Clarence & Mary Webster. Mayme attended and graduated from Kinloch High School in Kinloch MO.

Mayme Metcalf 2010

By 1952, she moved to East St Louis IL to embarked on a new journey in hairstyling and beauty while attending Muriel Davis School of Cosmetology. Because of her skillful and dynamic flair for perfecting the latest hairstyles, she quickly became the "go-to" stylist in town. After graduating from Muriel Davis School of Cosmetology, she opened her own salon in 1960 becoming the most "sought-after" and talented stylist. After 57 years of creating her magic, the "Checkerboard Style" was her favorite style of all time.

She is also an avid traveler who has crossed the globe - while seeking adventure, happiness and truly living while enjoying life to the fullest. She has traveled to Alaska, Jamaica, California, Colorado, Georgia, Kansas City, Las Vegas, and Mexico. These are just some of the many places Mayme has traveled. Her next destination is just a packed suitcase away.

Footstep Prayer:
So, journey the road you are traveling
Be grateful and richly blessed Remember that
God loves you Be still and let Him do the
<u>rest.</u>

Leon Anderson Wedding Day

Stan, Celeste, D'era & Kevin with Bill

Celeste, Jerome, Allen and Sandra

Sandra

Jerome and Sandra

Published 12 Days before Christmas

Author Celeste Berry-Barnes with husband Stan and daughter D'era

Congratulations Celeste!

Traveled to Carson, Compton, Redondo Beach,
Los Angeles and Palmdale CA

Visiting the Cosey family in LA

Erinn (Redd) & Lourenzy (Dude) Cosey

Los Angeles California

Erinn & Lourenzy Cosey

Beautiful Los Angeles Mountains

Los Angeles

Leaving Los Angeles

Arrived @Las Vegas Airport

Las Vegas Nevada

Little Rock and Hot Springs Arkansas

Touring Hot Spring Arkansas with sister
Bertha and nephew Charles Stanley

Hot Spring Arkansas

Historic Arlington Hotel and Spa

Largest hotel in Arkansas since 1875 with almost 500 rooms & suites – truly an American Treasure!

Hot Spring Water fountain and Bath House

Preserving Our Heritage

Known locally as the "Libbey," this building originally housed the 3rd Government Free Bathhouse and Public Health Service Clinic within the Hot Springs Reservation/National Park. This facility opened in 1922 to treat patients who were not able to pay for baths prescribed by their physician. Many of the patients needed treatment for venereal diseases, which prompted the Public Health Service to open a clinic for these specific treatments. The clinic relocated to the nearby Camp Garraday Transient Camp in 1948. The Government Free Bathhouse closed in 1957.

In 1958, the Physical Medicine Center opened in the bathhouse as a concessioner of the National Park Service. Hot Springs businessmen had urged then Park Superintendent Donald S. Libbey to provide the building for use as a physical therapy facility. In 1960 the building was renamed the Libbey Memorial Physical Medicine Center in his honor. Responding again to changes in the bathing business, the Hot Springs Health Spa was added on the upper floor in 1981. The concessions operations ended in December 2005.

Today, the National Park Service is making major repairs to the Libbey to insure the preservation of the building. In the future, Hot Springs National Park will offer the Libbey for lease, to be managed by the private sector.

Hot Spring Arkansas

Dallas Airport

Kevin and D'era

In route to Bozeman Montana, Idaho and Portland Oregon while traveling like a King in this Cadillac Escalade

Bill with Kevin (his co-pilot) traveling with Margret and D'era

Airbnb Pray Montana

Visited Little Church in Pray Montana

Little Chapel inside little Church and Bill signing the register

truck hauling potatoes

This truck was right in front of us. Not one Idaho potato fell off the truck

D'era, Kevin, Bill and Margret at Yellowstone National Park – Wyoming Montana that provided fantastic views

Kevin & D'era

Liberty Cap @Yellowstone Park

A Hot Spring

Kevin and D'era

Back on the Road again…

On the Road to Idaho…

Margret & Bill

Portland Oregon

Inside Portland Mall

Shopping in Portland Oregon

Portland deer in front yard

From the streets of Portland Oregon

Portland OR homeless

Portland Metro train

view of Portland downtown

Portland Bridge

Portland OR

exotic berries

Kevin & Bill find more species of berries

Good bye Portland!

Air flight back to St Louis

The Home of Superman

James Brown Statue Augusta GA
Say it Loud "I'm Black and Proud"

Arrived @Las Vegas Airport

Fun in Las Vegas with Pero and Shirlin Two Beautiful Souls

Flamingo Las Vegas

Leaving Las Vegas Airport

Old-Timers Attire in Branson

Maple Creek Branson MO

Air force Jets in Veteran's Museum

*The Branson Memorial Museum displays the history of the
20th century American Military conflicts. A testament to
the men and women who defended American freedom.*

Branson *Military* Memorial

Buffalo Soldiers

Bob Daniel tells the stories of the Buffalo Soldiers

The Buffalo Soldiers were members of the 10th Cavalry Regiment of the United States Army formed in 1866. The American Plains Indians referred to the black cavalry as "buffalo soldiers" because of their dark, curly hair which resembled a buffalo's coat and their fierce nature of fighting.

Real Buffalo Soldiers

Buffalo Solders traveled by Bicycles

Antique Car in Branson @ Capital Vacations

Mountain views leaving Branson MO

The Cross

This cross is 214 feet tall (off Hwy 65) in Walnut Shade MO – Just outside of Branson see this monument that was inspired by Kerry Brown who said that the Lord wanted this done. There is a door at the foot of the cross to give people an opportunity to enter in the Kingdom of God.

O'Fallon MO and Chicago IL

Traveling with Bill to O'Fallon MO celebrating sister's weekend with Mary, Wilma, Margret & Bertha

Chicago weekend with Sisters

Welcome to Florida

Key West and Miami

WOW! Arch in Miami Florida

First Arch for the city of Miami Gardens

Free People of Color Museum

Story-teller @
Free People of Color Museum

Free People of Color Art

New Orleans Riverwalk

Washington Monument in Ridgeland Mississippi

Bay St Louis Mississippi

St Rose de lima Catholic Church

This historic church is 100 years old in Bay St Louis Mississippi. This church was built under the direction of Elder Joe Labat (contractor and craftsman) for African Americans. Joan Thomas historian) noted that it was "pretty amazing" that Labat roses to the status of architect.

Inside St Rose de Lima Church

Joan Thomas explains that the mural's black Christ
reflect the Afro-centric nature of the church.

Inside St Rose de lima Church

Angels with No Face

The Mississippi Sound

The Mississippi Sound

From Home

The Best New Orleans Gumbo

Cape Kennedy
Cruise Ship

New Orleans Cruise

Caesars Superdome New Orleans LA

Museum honoring nationally acclaimed folk artist, humorist, and story-teller Alice Latimer Moseley

Agricultural Museum

Jackson Mississippi

Aspire to Inspire by D'era

Elvis Presley Statue

Memphis TN

The home of Elvis Presley @Graceland, BB King, Al Green, Beale Street, Blues Hall of Fame and Stax Museum, National Civil Right Museum and the Slave Haven Railroad.

Now back at the Ranch in Foley MO

This is Mubo and Tonto on the Ranch

Bill's Farm horses

I pray that you have found this little book inspirational – now share it with a friend to help them discover themselves and walk in faith with the confidence and assurance of God's love.

"….. be thou Faithful until death and I will give thee a crown of life!" – Rev 2:10

Well done, my good and faithful servant! – Matt 25:23

Traveling with William H Anderson Jr.

Traveling with Bill gives me overwhelming joy where our destiny intervened! He has a compassionate soul and warm heart. He is a graduate from Winfield High School. He also attended St Louis University. Performed Six Years of Military Service in the U.S. Air Force.

And worked 25 years at Washington University in St Louis Missouri.

About the Author and Poet

Margret V. Oglesby attended Arkansas Baptist College in Little Rock Arkansas for two years, and later earned her Bachelor of Arts degree from the University of Missouri St. Louis in Sociology. She founded "Stepping Out on Faith Production" in 1995 working with untapped talent of inner-city youth in St. Louis, Missouri. She has worked in the corporate industry for over 25 years, and 16 years in a financial institution. However, her true passion is writing and poetry since 1980. She said, "There were times in my life that I felt that God was not with me. I believe that these are the times that He wanted me to grow in faith." As she stepped out on faith on her own personal journey, God revealed to her the seven steps of faith. My greatest accomplishment was learning to depend on God and letting Him take full control of my life. Sometimes on your journey, you might feel you have taken a backstep, however be encouraged for there is one constant truth: God is always with you on the journey. Keep the Faith & Always Travel with God!

Margret attends Christ the King United UCC – Florissant Missouri under the spiritual guidance of *Pastor Dr Timica Emerson*

Margret Oglesby traveling with William Anderson Jr.

www.ingramcontent.com/pod-product-compliance
Lightning Source LLC
Chambersburg PA
CBHW051155120626
46547CB00012B/1065